1
Land Ahoy!

Nine-year-old Robin Newman was freezing cold. He was also soaking wet and very scared. Robin was the cabin boy on the *Golden Hind*, his uncle Francis's ship. Tonight's storm was the worst he'd ever seen. Angry waves splashed his face. He held on to the ropes around the bottom of a mast, choking on sea water.

The howling wind rattled the ship's sails like a ghost. It was so loud that Robin thought that the ship itself was going to break up.

Robin tried to cover his ears.
He didn't want to hear the cries
of the frightened crew. He watched
Old Jack, the ship's cook, praying
to God for help.

The very next morning, after weeks of storms, the winds suddenly dropped. The ship was safe and everyone, including the Captain put their hands together in thankful prayer. To the crew, it seemed like a miracle.

Robin's uncle's voice rang out over the deck of the ship. "Praise be to God that our lives have been spared."

"Do you know where we are, Sir?" asked an officer.

"Yes and no!" laughed General Francis Drake. "The gales have blown us far beyond the Straits of Magellan. But I will study the compass and set our course to the north at last."

"Be brave and proud, everyone,"
he cried. "We are the first Englishmen
to sail the Pacific Ocean!"

Robin was very proud of his uncle,
even though the other sailors did tease
him about it.

"Here he comes," the cook sometimes joked. "Who'd have thought the nephew of Francis Drake would try to pinch one of me ship's biscuits?"

And, after the storm, ship's biscuits was all there was left to eat.

One day the General summoned Robin to the deck.

"Look, Boy, the frigate bird!" his uncle cried. "And you know what that means... Bring me my pens and charts."

Robin obeyed instantly. Then he watched the bird snatch a fish from another bird's beak in mid-flight.

He remembered that frigate birds always returned to rest on land not sea.

"Land ahoy!" shrieked sharp-eyed Kit from the top of the main mast. "Land ahoy!"

The crew was so excited. They
began dancing round the deck. Even
Old Jack joined in, banging a spoon
on a bucket.

"Boy!" Drake ordered. "Fetch some wine from my cabin. This calls for a celebration."

"We shall be like the pirate frigate bird," the proud General promised his crew. "We'll seize the Spanish treasures."

"Aye," an officer grinned, "they've had things their own way for too long in the Pacific."

"Let them fear the name of Francis Drake!" the General boasted.

Solemnly he lifted his golden wine goblet and said, "We do all this, men, for the glory of God and for England, in the name of Her Majesty, Queen Elizabeth!"

Young Robin drank his glass of wine in one great gulp. It made a nice change from the stale beer that he and the crew were usually given.

2
Arise, Sir Francis!

The people on the shore fled to the
hills in terror when they saw the
Golden Hind drop anchor in Salada Bay.

"They're frightened of me already!"
laughed Francis Drake. "Come, let's
refill our larders and water barrels
from their stores."

The ship's carpenters and sail makers began to repair the storm damage to the *Golden Hind*. And the Captain rowed ashore with some of the ship's crew.

There was no one in the town, so Francis Drake ordered his men to collect supplies for the ship.

That evening Robin served his uncle a feast of spiced pork, fish and cheese.

He heard the Captain joking with his officers. "I'm told that the Spaniards think I'm a wizard!" he said. "They say I have a magic mirror which lets me see their ships from far away."

Robin kept dreaming about the magic mirror. He searched everywhere for it, but found nothing.

As the months went by, Robin watched his uncle lead many raids on the Spanish harbours. The General also attacked Spanish treasure ships in the Pacific Ocean. Robin was amazed at all the heavy gold and jewels that they loaded into the ship's hold.

"No need to look so worried, Boy, I'll make sure we don't sink," the General chuckled.

Further north, Drake went ashore again to explore. "I name this land New Albion," he announced. "It now belongs to Queen Elizabeth."

"How do we get home from here?"
Robin asked shyly.

"We shall head westwards across
the ocean," Drake said. "God willing,
Boy, we shall sail right around the
world back to England. We'll draw
our own maps on the way."

Ten weeks later, the *Golden Hind* reached the Spice Islands. By now many of the crew were sick with scurvy. But the General refused to stop exploring.

Expensive spices were crammed into the hold. The heavy ship set sail once more, but then…

Disaster struck! The ship stuck fast on a rocky reef. First they threw the cannons overboard, then some of the gold. But the ship still wouldn't move.

Then, some of the spices were tossed overboard. The sea changed colour and bubbled with pepper, nutmeg and cloves. But the ship stood still.

"It's no good, General, we're
doomed!" cried Old Jack, falling
on his knees to pray.

"Quiet, old man!" the General
ordered, pulling the cook off his knees.
"See, the wind's changed direction.
It's filling the sails again. With a bit
of luck, we'll escape."

And as he spoke, the ship slid off the reef and floated free. They were safe after all.

Robin was twelve years old when the *Golden Hind* eventually arrived in Plymouth, one September day in 1580. The local people had last seen the ship three years ago. They gave Francis Drake, a Devon man himself, a hero's welcome home.

The following spring, the *Golden Hind* sailed triumphantly up the River Thames to London. There Robin had the honour of serving Queen Elizabeth when she came to dine on deck with his uncle. Robin watched them proudly.

"Many thanks for all the gifts from your travels," Her Majesty smiled. "Now hand me your sword and kneel down," the Queen commanded Francis.

Queen Elizabeth touched his shoulders lightly with the sword.

"Arise *Sir* Francis Drake!" she announced grandly. "The first Englishman to sail around the world!"

3
Eight years later

"Robin, take charge of loading the ship," Sir Francis said to his nephew. It was Friday, the 19th of July, 1588, Robin Newman's twentieth birthday. Now one of his uncle's most trusted officers, Robin celebrated the day by preparing for battle against the Spanish Armada!

Robin leaned over the starboard side of the General's flagship, the *Revenge*. He made sure that the ship was properly loaded.

Soon the Queen's ships were full
of supplies and ready to meet the
enemy. This was just as well because
the look-outs had spotted a huge fleet
of Spanish ships a long way off in the
distance. A line of beacon fires were
lit along the coast to warn of the
Armada's slow, steady advance up
the English Channel. Robin hurried
to report the news to his uncle.

He found Sir Francis Drake, the
new Vice-Admiral of the Queen's
Navy, calmly playing bowls.

Sir Francis stroked his beard and winked at him. "Fear not, Robin," he smiled. "There's time yet to finish this game of bowls, and then beat the Spanish!"

Sir Francis knew there was no need to rush. The south-west wind would make it difficult to get the ships out of Plymouth harbour until high tide.

Robin enjoyed listening to the sailors
as he headed back through the streets.

"Heard what the General said?"
cackled one seaman. "He's afraid o'
nothin'. There's no way we can lose
with captains like him."

It was Robin's job to beat the ship's
large drum, to call up the sailors from
the town... Drake's Drum, everyone
called it.

With extra barrels of gunpowder, food and water loaded aboard, the English ships set out during the night. Next morning Robin saw the vast Spanish Armada in full sail... over 130 galleons, each as tall as a castle.

"Aye, we may be outnumbered, Robin," Sir Francis said grimly, "but our gallant ships are swifter!"

There were fierce clashes all along the south coast over the next few days. But Sir Francis Drake and his brave men had to stop the Armada from landing on English soil at all costs.

The *Revenge* was always in the
thick of the action. The General's face
and white silk shirt were streaked
with sweat and dirt as he worked
on deck with his crew.

At last the Armada headed to the
French port of Calais to get extra help.

Sir Francis took Robin to an urgent meeting on board the Lord High Admiral's *Ark Royal* to discuss what they should do next.

"Let's use fireships!" the General advised forcefully. "That will put the fear into them. But we can't afford to wait. We must strike before it is too late."

So Robin helped prepare the 200-tonne *Thomas*. It was filled with bundles of twigs, covered with tar and then steered towards the Armada. Robin escaped in a rowing boat after lighting the fuses.

At midnight on the last Sunday
in July, several burning ships drifted
on the tide toward the Spanish fleet.
In terror, the Spaniards cut their
anchor cables and tried to get away.

Robin even saw some sailors jumping
for their lives into the frothing waves.

"There's a storm brewing up!" cried
Robin. "They won't be able to escape
along the Channel now!"

That day the Armada lost several galleons. Not one English ship was sunk in the battle, but both sides were low on ammunition.

"That's enough, we'll let nature do the rest," the General decided. "The gales will wreck a lot more of their ships as they try to get round our rocky coasts back to Spain."

When the *Revenge* arrived home to
Plymouth, everyone was talking about
Sir Francis Drake's victory. And Robin
had a few tales of his own to tell.

Robin was proud of his Uncle.
But he was even more proud to have
sounded Drake's Drum and called
up so many brave English sailors.